W0017902

Entrepreneurship Snapshots 2010

Measuring the Impact of the Financial Crisis on New Business Registration

THE WORLD BANK
Washington, D.C.

© 2011 The International Bank for Reconstruction and Development / The World Bank
1818 H Street NW
Washington DC 20433
Telephone: 202-473-1000
Internet: www.worldbank.org

All rights reserved

1 2 3 4 13 12 11 10

This volume is a product of the staff of the International Bank for Reconstruction and Development / The World Bank. The findings, interpretations, and conclusions expressed in this volume do not necessarily reflect the views of the Executive Directors of The World Bank or the governments they represent.

The World Bank does not guarantee the accuracy of the data included in this work. The boundaries, colors, denominations, and other information shown on any map in this work do not imply any judgement on the part of The World Bank concerning the legal status of any territory or the endorsement or acceptance of such boundaries.

Rights and Permissions
The material in this publication is copyrighted. Copying and/or transmitting portions or all of this work without permission may be a violation of applicable law. The International Bank for Reconstruction and Development / The World Bank encourages dissemination of its work and will normally grant permission to reproduce portions of the work promptly.

For permission to photocopy or reprint any part of this work, please send a request with complete information to the Copyright Clearance Center Inc., 222 Rosewood Drive, Danvers, MA 01923, USA; telephone: 978-750-8400; fax: 978-750-4470; Internet: www.copyright.com.

All other queries on rights and licenses, including subsidiary rights, should be addressed to the Office of the Publisher, The World Bank, 1818 H Street NW, Washington, DC 20433, USA; fax: 202-522-2422; e-mail: pubrights@worldbank.org.

ISBN: 978-0-8213-8476-3
eISBN: 978-0-8213-8637-8
DOI: 10.1596/978-0-8213-8476-3

Library of Congress Cataloging-in-Publication Data

Entrepreneurship snapshots 2010 : measuring the impact of the financial crisis on new business registration.
    p. cm.
 ISBN 978-0-8213-8476-3
 1. Entrepreneurship. 2. New business enterprises. 3. Financial crises. I. World Bank.
 HB615.E634658 2011
    338'.04—dc22

                                    2010041011

Cover design: Critical Stages

Contents

Map

Preface

The 2010 World Bank Group *Entrepreneurship Snapshots* (WBGES) provides a unique indicator of new business registration around the world that can be used to study the factors that foster dynamic private sector growth. Now in its fourth year, the WBGES measures entrepreneurial activity in 112 developing and high-income economies over the period 2004–09. The data offer a distinctive and timely snapshot of the impact of the 2008 financial crisis on entrepreneurial activity.

There is wide variation in new business registration across economies. On average, in high-income economies about four new firms register every year for every 1,000 working-age adults; in low- and middle-income economies, the figure is less than one new firm per 1,000 working-age adults. The data show that more dynamic business creation occurs in countries that provide entrepreneurs with a stable legal and regulatory regime, a rapid and inexpensive business registration process, more flexible employment regulations, and low corporate taxes. The data also show that nearly all economies experienced a sharp drop in business registration during the crisis. This drop is more pronounced in economies with higher levels of financial development and economies more affected by the crisis.

The results in the WBGES can help guide effective policy making and deliver new capabilities for identifying the impact of reforms. Future WBGES editions will shed light on the pace of recovery in new business registrations following the crisis.

Acknowledgments

This report was prepared by a team led by Leora Klapper and Inessa Love and made up of Elena Cirmizi, Caroline Giraud, and Douglas Randall. Anat Lewin contributed to the section on modernizing the business registration process.

The report team is grateful for the valuable comments provided by colleagues across the World Bank Group. Special thanks go to Asli Demirgüc-Kunt, Cecile Fruman, Andrei Mikhnev, Juan Manuel Quesada Delgado, and E. J. Reedy.

This project was developed in collaboration with and financially supported by the Ewing Marion Kauffman Foundation, Investment Climate Advisory Services (the International Finance Corporation and the World Bank), and the Development Research Group (the World Bank).

Overview

Business owners and would-be entrepreneurs are often at the mercy of macroeconomic conditions. This was never more true than in 2008 and 2009, when the financial crisis reverberated throughout the global economic system following the failure of several U.S. and Western European banking institutions. The first phase of the crisis affected mainly the United States, the United Kingdom, and other developed countries. After the collapse of Lehman Brothers, in September 2008, the crisis rapidly spread around the globe, reaching even the most remote destinations. Markets plummeted, global trade collapsed, and millions of people were left unemployed.

Most financial institutions were adversely affected, either directly, through their connections with failed banks, or indirectly, through interbank credit market linkages. In addition, policy measures aimed at tightening the regulatory requirements on capital made banks reluctant to lend. As a result, a severe credit crunch developed, and even the largest borrowers experienced tightening of their financial access. The credit crunch resulted in firms reducing their investment, cutting back on research and development, and passing up attractive new projects (Campello, Graham, and Campbell 2009).

New businesses are likely to have been even more severely affected by the crisis than mature businesses Even in non-crisis times, new and young firms tend to be more constrained than older firms which often have established reputations and enjoy easier access to finance (Chavis, Klapper, and Love 2010). Given the sudden scarcity of credit and the uncertain economic outlook, it is reasonable to assume that that entrepreneurs wanting to start a new business or register an existing informal business were hit especially hard by the downturn. Until now, however there has been a lack of comprehensive evidence to support this assumption.

New data from the 2010 World Bank Group *Entrepreneurship Snapshots* (WBGES), a longitudinal study of entrepreneurial activity in 112 economies, allow the impact of the financial crisis on new business registration worldwide to be studied for the first time. These data, presented here, also allow for the cross-economy longitudinal study of entrepreneurial activity that assesses the determinants of formal business creation and its relationship to business environment and economic growth.

The impact of the 2008–09 financial crisis on new business creation should be of special interest given the importance of entrepreneurs and young firms to the continued dynamism of the modern market economy; it is well established that a robust entry rate of new business can foster competition and economic growth (Djankov and others 2002; Klapper, Laeven, and Rajan 2006). In the United States, for instance, young jobs were an important source of net job creation between 1980 and 2005 (Haltiwanger, Jarmin, and Miranda 2009; Stangler and Litan 2009). As policy makers and business leaders worldwide seek to restart the engines of economic growth in the wake of the crisis, they may find a renewed focus on entrepreneurship to be particularly valuable. In this vein, the 2010 WBGES offers a timely contribution to the study of new business creation.

Now in its fourth year, the WBGES was established in 2004 as a biennial complement to the World Bank's *Doing Business* database, which provides annual measures of the business environment that now span 41 indicators and 183 economies, enabling policy makers, business leaders, and researchers to trace the evolution of the business environment in a given economy and compare indicators across a range of diverse economies. The WBGES provides an internationally comparable metric for exploring the relationship between the *Doing Business* indicators and the number of newly registered firms. As both *Doing Business* and WBGES data are collected over time, it is possible to evaluate the impact of reforms on new business registration.

The 2010 WBGES includes data on the number of limited liability firms in 112 economies that registered for the first time between 2004 and 2009. Data were collected directly from the registrar of companies, the entry point for entrepreneurs joining or transitioning to the formal sector.[1] The 2010 WBGES builds on earlier editions of the data and incorporates improvements in methodology and increased participation by low-income countries, notably those in Sub-Saharan Africa. As outlined in the second section of the report, the data use the same unit of measurement used by *Doing Business*. Because of constraints on data availability, the WBGES covers only the formal business sector, even though informal businesses make up a large share of the economy in less developed countries.

The main variable of interest is the density of new business entry, defined as the number of newly registered limited liability companies per 1,000 working-age (15–64) people.[2] The data allow researchers to explore the relationship between the business environment and new firm creation, as well as assess the impact of the 2008–09 financial crisis on entrepreneurship.

This report summarizes the first analysis of the WBGES data. It focuses on the following questions:

1. How does firm creation vary around the world, in particular with the level of economic and financial development?

2. What is the relationship between entrepreneurship and the business environment?

3. How did the financial crisis affect entrepreneurial activity in the formal sector?

4. What factors determine how severely the crisis affected new firm creation?

With respect to the first question, the data show wide variation in new entry across countries. Rates of business registrations are significantly correlated with the level of development in a country: the average entry density is 4.21 in high-income countries, 2.43 in upper-middle-income countries, 0.77 in lower-middle-income countries, and 0.33 in low-income countries (figure 1).[3] This means that on average there are about four new firms registered every year per 1,000 people in industrial countries and less than one new firm registered per 1,000 people in low- and lower-middle-income countries.

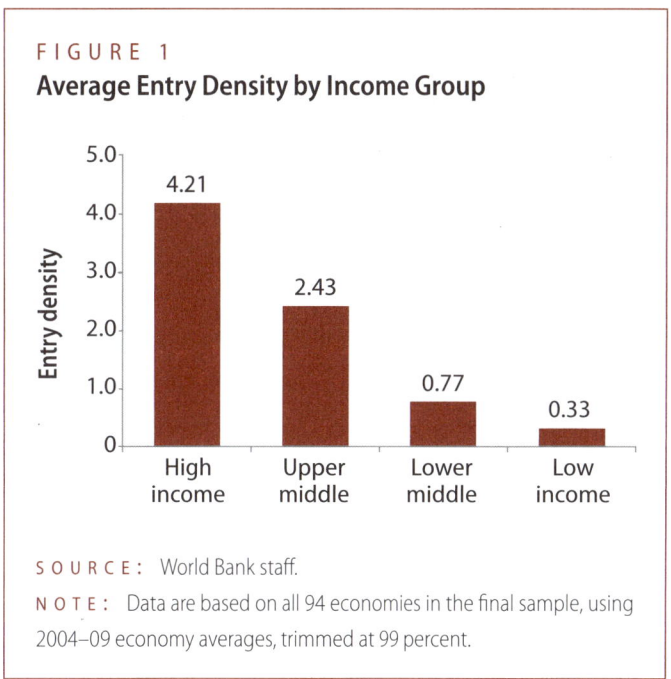

FIGURE 1

Average Entry Density by Income Group

S O U R C E : World Bank staff.

N O T E : Data are based on all 94 economies in the final sample, using 2004–09 economy averages, trimmed at 99 percent.

The data also show a strong positive relationship between entry density and the development of financial markets: countries with more developed financial markets experience a higher volume of registrations because finance is more widely available to support new businesses.

With respect to the second question, the data show that various components of a country's business environment are significant indicators of new firm registrations, even after controlling for the overall level of economic development. As a summary measure of the various business environment indicators in a country, the *Doing Business* data show countries' overall ranks. These ranks can be used as a measure of business environment quality. Figure 2 shows the strong positive correlation between a country's overall rank in *Doing Business* and entry density.

These results suggest that dynamic business creation occurs in countries that provide entrepreneurs with good governance, a strong legal and regulatory environment, and reduced red tape. As the section below on regulation and governance shows, significant relationships exist between entry density and the ease of starting a business (expressed as the cost of registration, the number of days required to start a business, and the number of procedures required); country-level governance; and the corporate tax rate.

The section of the report on modernization of business registration processes examines the recent trend toward modernization of the business registration process. It shows that using the Internet to register a business allows for faster and cheaper registration, even when only part of the process is handled online. As a result, entry density is also higher in countries with modernized registries. These results are consistent with earlier work on the efficient allocation of inputs and other resources to entrepreneurial activities (Jovanovic 1982) and the impact of regulatory reform and institutional quality (Demirgüc-Kunt, Love, and Maksimovic 2006; Mullainathan and Schnabl 2009).

Regarding the third question, time-series data provide a snapshot of the impact of the 2008–09 global financial crisis on new firm creation. Data for the final sample of 94 countries show that nearly all economies experienced a sharp drop in business entry during the crisis (figure 3). Only 20 percent of countries experienced growth in business entry between 2008 and 2009, down from 74 percent between 2006 and 2007. With the onset of the financial crisis, new business creation slowed, first in advanced

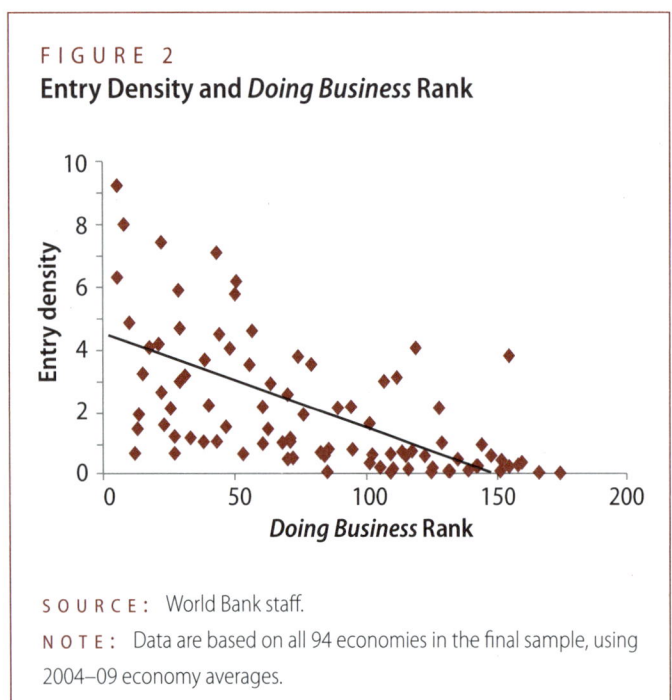

FIGURE 2
Entry Density and *Doing Business* Rank

SOURCE: World Bank staff.
NOTE: Data are based on all 94 economies in the final sample, using 2004–09 economy averages.

economies and then in the rest of the world, paralleling the spread of the crisis.

Regarding the fourth question, the data show that countries with more developed financial markets experienced larger contractions in new firm creation, most likely because of the credit crunch that has characterized this crisis. Withdrawals of finance tend to have a large impact on start-ups when finance plays a larger role in economic activity. However, financial development is important for business creation. In addition, the degree to which the crisis affected new firm creation is correlated with measures of crisis severity: countries that suffered more severe crises also had the largest drops in new registrations, as discussed below.

The new data set fills the gaps that existed until now in entrepreneurial activity around the world. Earlier cross-economy measurements of entrepreneurial activity are limited, but the data that do exist demonstrate that much can be learned about the relationship between entrepreneurship and economic growth through the development of longitudinal data sets (Wennekers and others 2005). Cross-economy data have been used to demonstrate a relationship between new firm creation and levels of economic development (van Stel, Carree, and Thurik 2005). Furthermore, from an evolutionary economics perspective, research

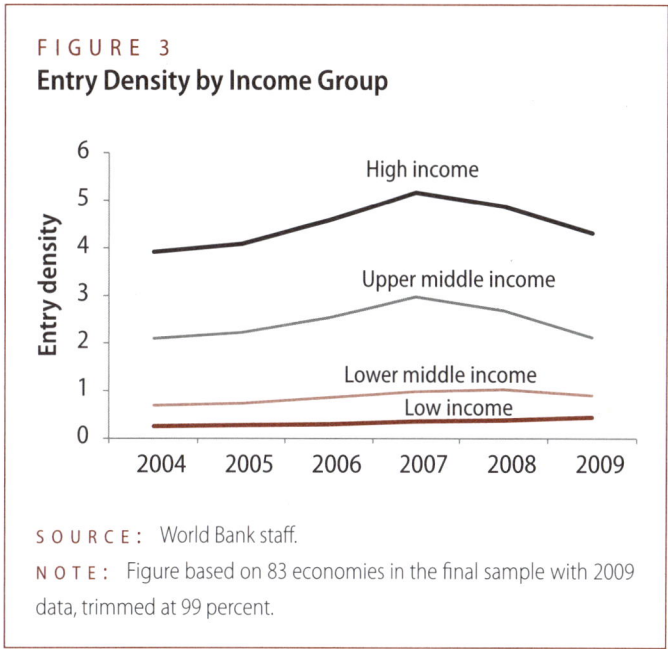

FIGURE 3
Entry Density by Income Group

SOURCE: World Bank staff.
NOTE: Figure based on 83 economies in the final sample with 2009 data, trimmed at 99 percent.

suggests that disparities in economic growth between advanced and developing economies can narrow as a result of the growth in entrepreneurial activity (Galor and Stelios 2006). At the country level, U.S. census data have been used to demonstrate that young firms, not small firms as is commonly believed, are the principal force behind net job creation (Haltiwanger, Jarmin, and Miranda 2009; Stangler and Litan 2009).

Several advances in the study of entrepreneurship have been made using the 2008 WBGES database. Klapper, Amit, and Guillen (2010) find significant relationships between entrepreneurial activity and indicators of economic and financial development and growth, the quality of legal and regulatory environment, and governance. Dutta, Roy, and Sobel (2009) use the 2008 WBGES database to demonstrate that media freedom has a large and significant positive impact on entrepreneurship across countries. Busch and Lassmann (2009) use the same data set to demonstrate a positive correlation between self-employment rates of U.S. immigrants and the degree of entrepreneurial activity in their countries of origin.

The WBGES database will be updated biennially for the foreseeable future.

Forthcoming editions of the database will provide insight into how the fiscal and monetary policies implemented by governments in response to the crisis affected the revival of new firm creation. It will also be possible to examine the precrisis financial and institutional characteristics that encouraged a rapid and strong recovery in new business registration in the wake of the crisis. This report hypothesizes that although economies with more developed financial markets were hit harder by the crisis, they will enjoy stronger and quicker recoveries in new firm creation.

Methodology

This section begins by defining entrepreneurship. It then describes the coverage, data sources, and sample selection used in the study.

Defining Entrepreneurship

In order to measure entrepreneurship in a way that is universally comparable, this study employs a methodology that can be applied across heterogeneous legal regimes and economic systems. Previous efforts have been made in this regard, but most of them focused solely on the developed world and did not take into account

differences in legal systems, sectors, and economic structures (UN 2005).

The concept of entrepreneurship lacks a common language. Joseph Schumpeter defines entrepreneurship as the assumption of risk and responsibility in designing and implementing a business strategy or starting a business (Schumpeter 1911). Gough (1969) defines an entrepreneur as a person who undertakes and operates a new enterprise and assumes some accountability for the inherent risks. For practitioners, entrepreneurship has generally been viewed as the process of creating new wealth. The entrepreneurial process centers on the discovery, creation, and profitable exploitation of markets for goods and services.[4] Therefore, for the purposes of the analysis in this study, entrepreneurship is defined as "the activities of an individual or a group aimed at initiating economic enterprise in the formal sector under a legal form of business."

It is important to create a standard unit of measurement. Generally, entrepreneurial activities are carried out by businesses. However, because of the lack of a universally agreed upon definition of what constitutes a business, economic, statistical, or legal definitions have been used. For instance, the United States bases its business statistics on establishments. Canada reports average labor units. Countries reporting to Eurostat and the United Nations Economic Commission on Europe use various measures, including legal (enterprises), geographical (local unit), and activity-based (kind of activity unit) measures for their business statistics.[5] The proposed unit of measurement must take into account the availability of the data, its consistency across countries, its relevance to entrepreneurship, and its focus on the formal sector.

The WGBES gathers data on corporations, defined as private companies with limited liability (the same definition used by the World Bank's *Doing Business* report). Limited liability corporations are the most prevalent business form in most economies. Limited liability is a concept in which the financial liability of the firm's members is limited to the value of their investment in the company. A limited liability corporation is a separate legal entity that has its own privileges and liabilities. Although the laws on business registration vary greatly across countries, the approach to legal entities is largely uniform: any business with a unique legal entity (or "corporate personhood") separate from its owners must be registered.[6] This study collects information on all corporations regardless of their economic or staff size, as in many economies neither financial information nor the number of employees is collected, making it impossible to identify firm size.

Coverage and Data Sources

This report builds on earlier WBGES data and incorporates improvements in methodology and increased participation by low-income countries, notably in Sub-Saharan Africa. In 2010, 112 economies participated in the survey—the highest coverage to date—including 20 first-time participants.[7]

Surveys requesting data on the number of newly registered limited liability firms were sent by email and fax to official government sources. In 70 percent of economies, surveys were completed and data provided directly by the registrar of companies, the government entity responsible for recording and maintaining information on new and existing firms. Data for other countries were collected from national statistical offices and chambers of commerce. In India data were purchased from D&B, because nationally representative business registry data on corporations were not otherwise available.[8]

Government officials completed either paper or electronic surveys. The database was checked for consistency across economies and over time. Quality assurance measures included comparing data with published official data or related country case studies.

Sample Selection

The 2010 WBGES is not a comprehensive study of all firms in the 112 economies surveyed. In order to provide an accurate and internationally relevant data analysis, certain exclusions were made at the firm and economy levels.

Firm-Level Selection

The selection of firms was based on several criteria. Each is described below.

Formal sector firms. This study is limited to the formal private sector. Firms that operate informally are excluded because business registries do not provide accurate tallies of these firms. The only way to enumerate firms in the informal sector is through economic censuses, which, because of their high costs, are infrequently conducted. The relevance of the informal sector to job creation, particularly in developing economies, is undeniable. The "shadow economy" is excluded only because of lack of data.

There is a strong and inverse relationship between the size of the informal economy (defined as percentage of GDP) and new business density (defined as the ratio of new firms to working-age population, scaled by 1,000). This relationship is shown in figure 4.

The literature highlights the potential advantages of formal sector participation, including police and judicial protection (and less vulnerability to corruption and the demand for bribes), access to formal credit institutions, the ability to use formal labor contracts, and greater access to foreign markets (Schneider and Enste 2000). Because firms that choose to remain informal are often subsistence-type businesses, they may be unable to realize their full growth potential. "High-growth" entrepreneurship is thus most likely to happen through formally registered firms. For example, of the more than 100,000 firms estimated to exist in Côte d'Ivoire, only about 4,000 are registered firms, but the formal sector accounts for more than 60 percent of GDP and 90 percent of value added (Klapper and Richmond 2009).

New firms. The database does not include the number of total or closed firms, because most countries do not accurately collect data on total active or inactive firms. The stock number of total firms may thus include many closed firms that did not formally deregister. Closure costs are generally low in high-income economies: in Norway and Singapore, for example, they represent less than 1 percent of the estate's value, as defined by *Doing Business*. In contrast, these costs can be significant in lower-income economies. In the Dominican Republic and Uganda, for example, closing costs exceed 30 percent of the estate's value (World Bank 2009a).

The process of removing inactive firms from the registry varies widely across countries. In Sweden, for example, firms are removed from the registry if they do not submit financial statements and an audited account within 11 months of the end of the financial year.[9] Austria and the Slovak Republic remove firms that fail to file financial reports for two consecutive years.[10] In other economies, such as Cambodia and Madagascar, formal firm closure mechanisms do not exist (World Bank 2009a). Consequently, only the number of newly registered firms (that

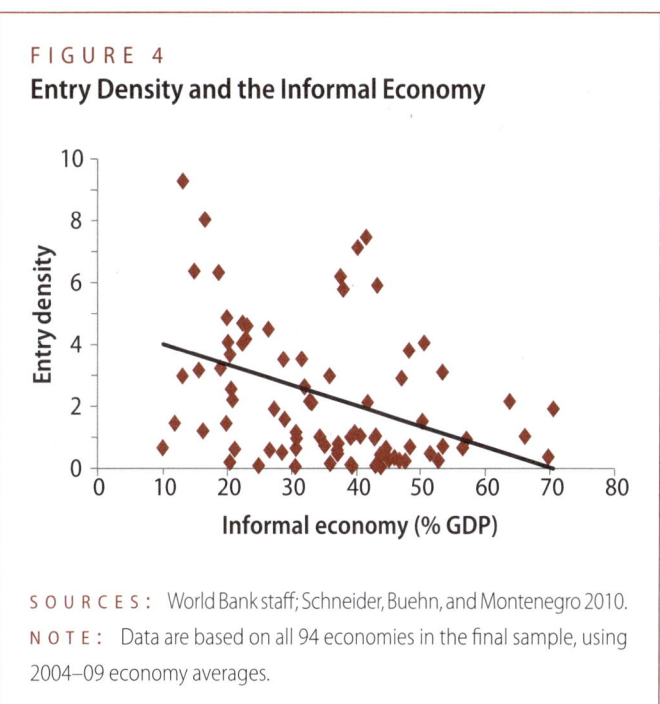

S O U R C E S :   World Bank staff; Schneider, Buehn, and Montenegro 2010.
N O T E :   Data are based on all 94 economies in the final sample, using 2004–09 economy averages.

is, the flow rather than the stock) is measured here. This exclusion prevents entry rates (new firms normalized by total firms) from being calculated.

Companies with limited liability. Partnerships and sole proprietorships are not considered, because these types of entities differ substantially with respect to their definition and regulation worldwide. Several legal systems (such as Peru's) do not require these entities to be registered for statistical or tax purposes.[11] The focus here is thus solely on limited liability companies (figure 5).

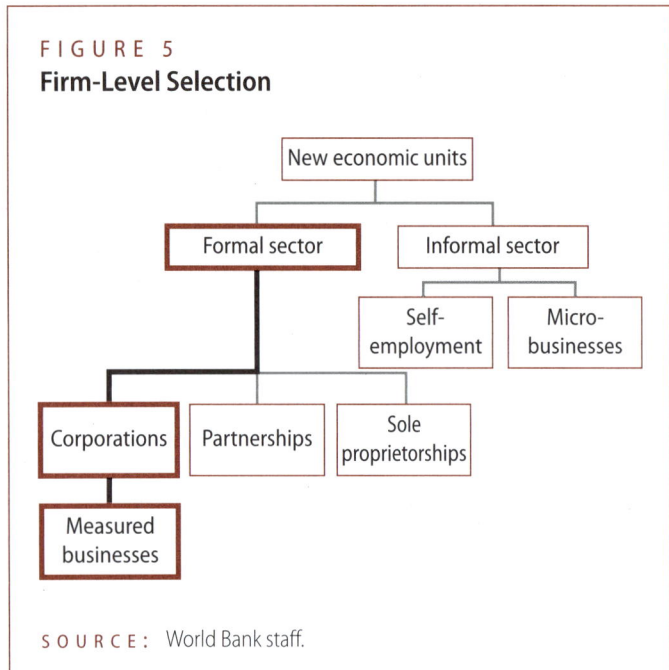

FIGURE 5
Firm-Level Selection

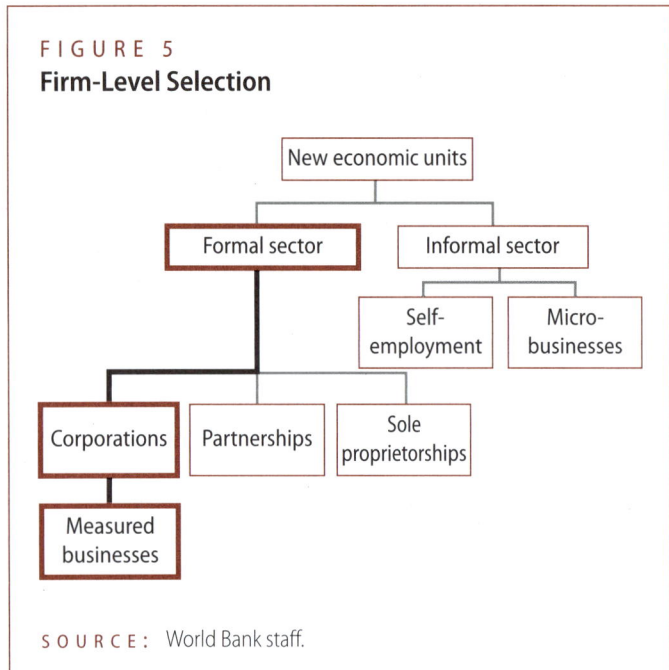

SOURCE: World Bank staff.

Economy-Level Selection

The selection of economies was based on several criteria. Each is described below.

Exclusion of offshore financial centers. Data collected from economies categorized by the International Monetary Fund and the Financial Stability Forum as offshore financial centers are excluded from the analysis, because registered entities in these countries may not fit the definition of entrepreneurship defined here (box 1).[12] The information provided by these economies likely reflects a nontrivial number of shell companies, defined as companies

BOX 1
Exclusion of Offshore Financial Centers

Offshore financial centers, generally in small economies, are excluded from the analysis because many of the new firms registered in these countries do not fit the definition of entrepreneurship. In 2008 average entry density (the number of new firms divided by the size of the working-age population) in 16 offshore centers excluding the British Virgin Islands was 13.8, compared with 2.4 in the rest of the world. If offshore financial centers were included, these economies, which together make up less than 1 percent of the total working-age population of the sample, would account for 8 percent of the new firms created in 2008.

The British Virgin Islands provides an extreme illustration of the distorting effects of offshore financial centers. In 2007 the country had 77,022 newly registered corporations—about four new firms for each working-age citizen. The average for industrial countries was about four new firms per 1,000 working-age citizens.

SOURCE: World Bank staff.

that are registered for tax purposes but are not active. Such corporations may be set up for illegal purposes, such as tax evasion, or formed in anticipation of attracting funding. They may also come into existence when a corporation has failed and its operations have ceased but its shell remains.

Technical/organizational limitations. Decentralization of business registries, lack of professional and technical resources, and inefficient legal support of the data collection process made the aggregation of the registration data at the national level impossible in some cases. Several countries do not collect data on newly created business or lack the tools or resources to process the data once collected. Some countries, such as Ethiopia, require firms to register with the national government only if they plan to do business outside of their regional borders. Other countries are unwilling to share their information. For this reason, many countries, mostly developing economies, are not included.

An additional caveat is necessary when examining data over time: events sometimes have a dramatic impact on new firm registration. Political crises, corruption scandals, and other external shocks can affect new business density (box 2). They have been accounted for when considering the time series data presented in the next section.

BOX 2
Effect of Political Events in Thailand

Political crises, corruption scandals, and other external shocks can affect the level of new business density. They should be accounted for when considering time series data.

In several economies, events dramatically affected new firm registration. New firm creation in Thailand grew at an average annual rate of 12 percent between 2000 and 2005. On September 19, 2006, a military junta overthrew the interim government and declared martial law, which lasted until January 2007. New firm creation dropped sharply between 2005 and 2007.

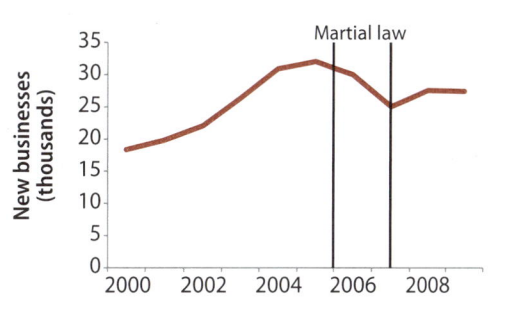

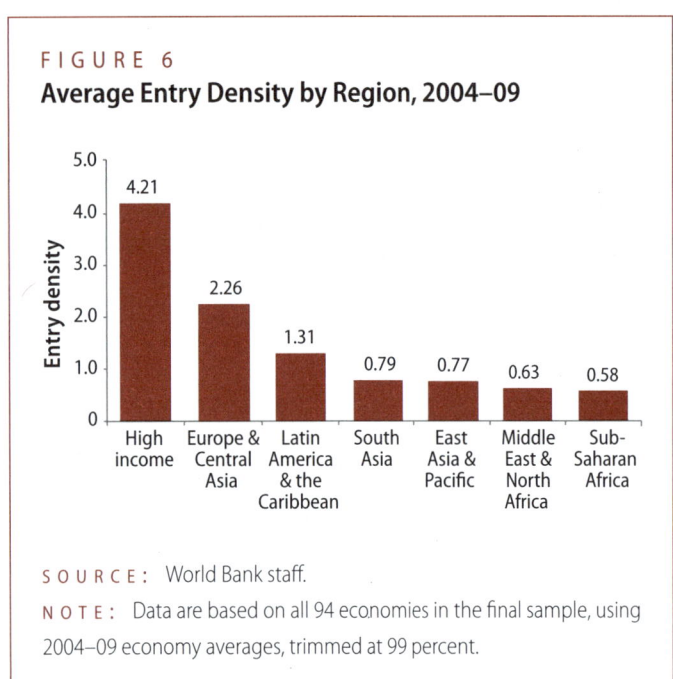

FIGURE 6

Average Entry Density by Region, 2004–09

SOURCE: World Bank staff.

NOTE: Data are based on all 94 economies in the final sample, using 2004–09 economy averages, trimmed at 99 percent.

The analysis focuses primarily on new business entry density, calculated as the number of newly registered firms as a percentage of the economy's working-age (15–64) population, normalized by 1,000. In order to maximize consistency and coverage, the analysis focuses on the period 2004–09 (see map). The appendix lists entry density by economy for this period.

The final sample of 94 economies reveals significant disparities across regions, ranging from an entry density of 0.58 in Sub-Saharan Africa to 4.21 in high-income economies (figure 6).[13] Figure 7 shows that entry density is significantly correlated with per capita GDP and financial development.

Entrepreneurship and the Business Environment

This section begins by examining four indicators of regulations and governance. It then examines the modernization of the business registration process.

Regulations and Governance

Four indicators from the World Bank's *Doing Business* report facilitate analysis of the impact of the business environment

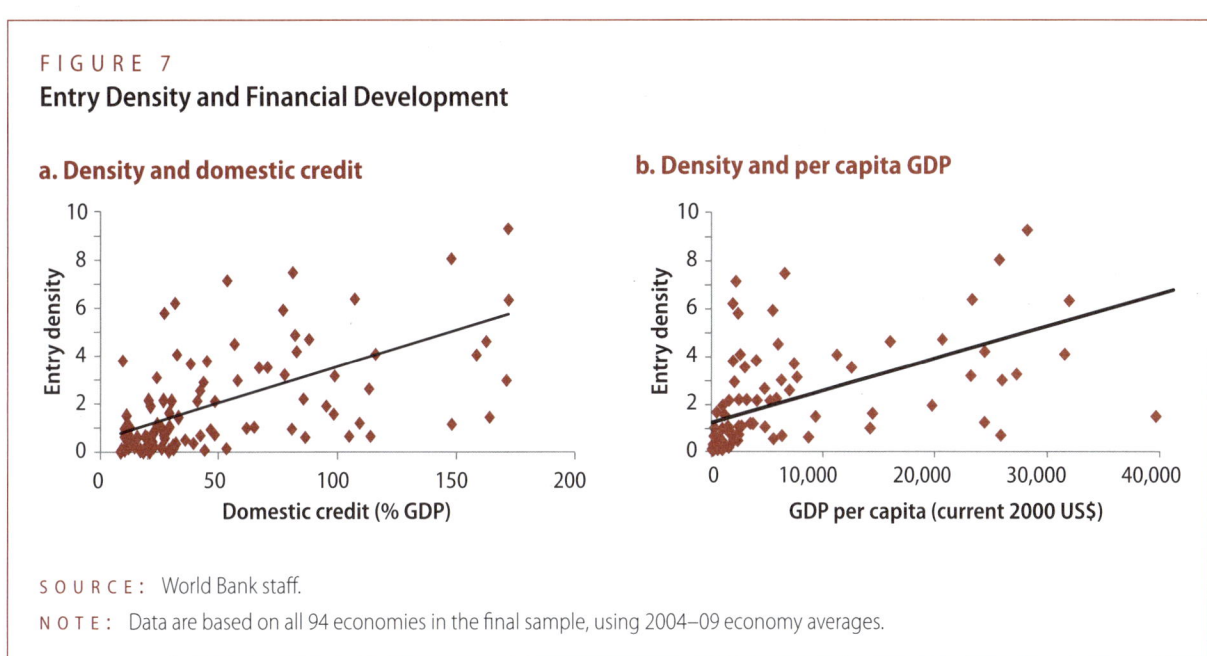

FIGURE 7

Entry Density and Financial Development

a. Density and domestic credit

Entry density

Domestic credit (% GDP)

b. Density and per capita GDP

Entry density

GDP per capita (current 2000 US$)

S O U R C E : World Bank staff.

N O T E : Data are based on all 94 economies in the final sample, using 2004–09 economy averages.

and barriers to entry on new firm creation. The first indicator, the cost of starting a business (measured as a percentage of the economy's per capita income), captures all official fees and fees for legal and professional services involved in incorporating a business (figure 8, panel a). The strong relationship between the cost of starting a business and new firm creation is also reflected in a case study from Germany (box 3).

The second and third indicators measure the time and the number of procedures necessary to start a business (figure 8, panels b and c). The fourth indicator, the cost of closing a business (measured as a percentage of the estate's value), includes court fees as well as fees of insolvency practitioners, independent assessors, lawyers, and accountants (figure 8, panel d).[14] Employment rigidity—a composite of subindexes on difficulty of hiring, rigidity of hours, and difficulty of redundancy—is highly correlated with all of the *Doing Business* measures as well as the variable of interest here, entry density.

A formal econometric analysis extends these simple correlations. To ensure that better business environment is related to subsequent business registration, cross-country regressions average new registrations over 2005–09, using the business

Average Entry Density by Economy, 2004–09

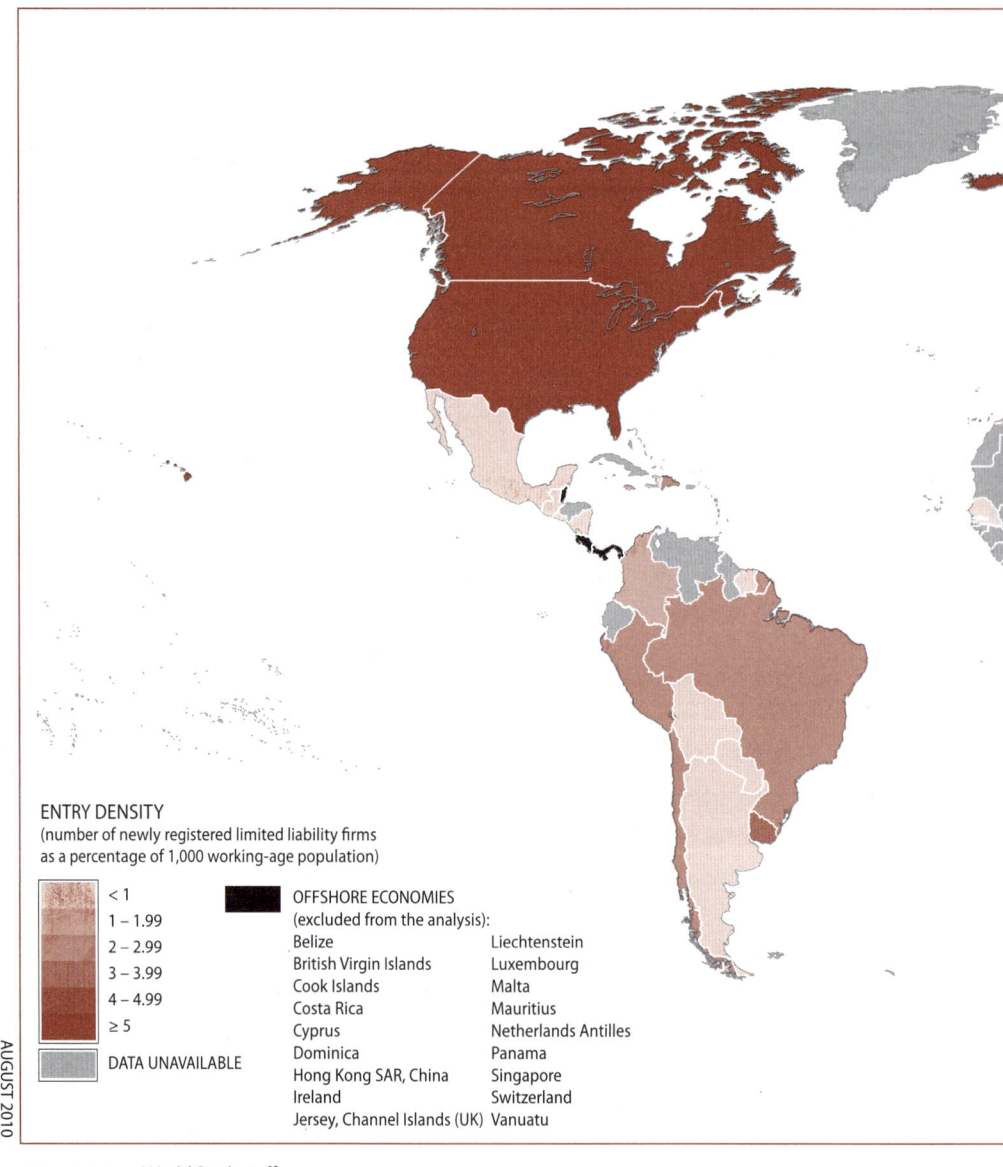

ENTRY DENSITY
(number of newly registered limited liability firms
as a percentage of 1,000 working-age population)

	< 1
	1 – 1.99
	2 – 2.99
	3 – 3.99
	4 – 4.99
	≥ 5
	DATA UNAVAILABLE

OFFSHORE ECONOMIES
(excluded from the analysis):

Belize	Liechtenstein
British Virgin Islands	Luxembourg
Cook Islands	Malta
Costa Rica	Mauritius
Cyprus	Netherlands Antilles
Dominica	Panama
Hong Kong SAR, China	Singapore
Ireland	Switzerland
Jersey, Channel Islands (UK)	Vanuatu

AUGUST 2010

S O U R C E :   World Bank staff.

N O T E :   Some countries use WBGES 2008 data (United States) or estimations (China).

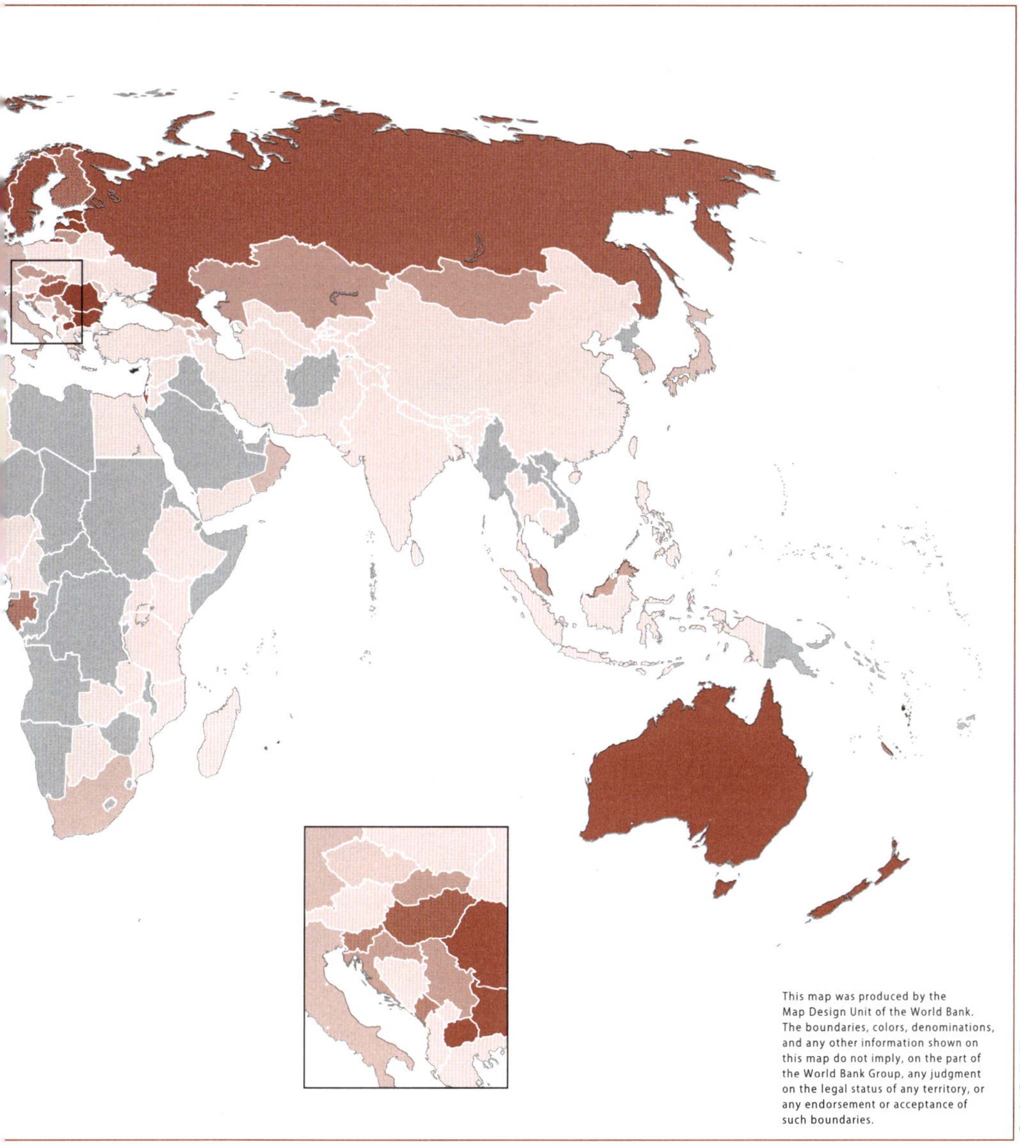

This map was produced by the
Map Design Unit of the World Bank.
The boundaries, colors, denominations,
and any other information shown on
this map do not imply, on the part of
the World Bank Group, any judgment
on the legal status of any territory, or
any endorsement or acceptance of
such boundaries.

IBRD 37975

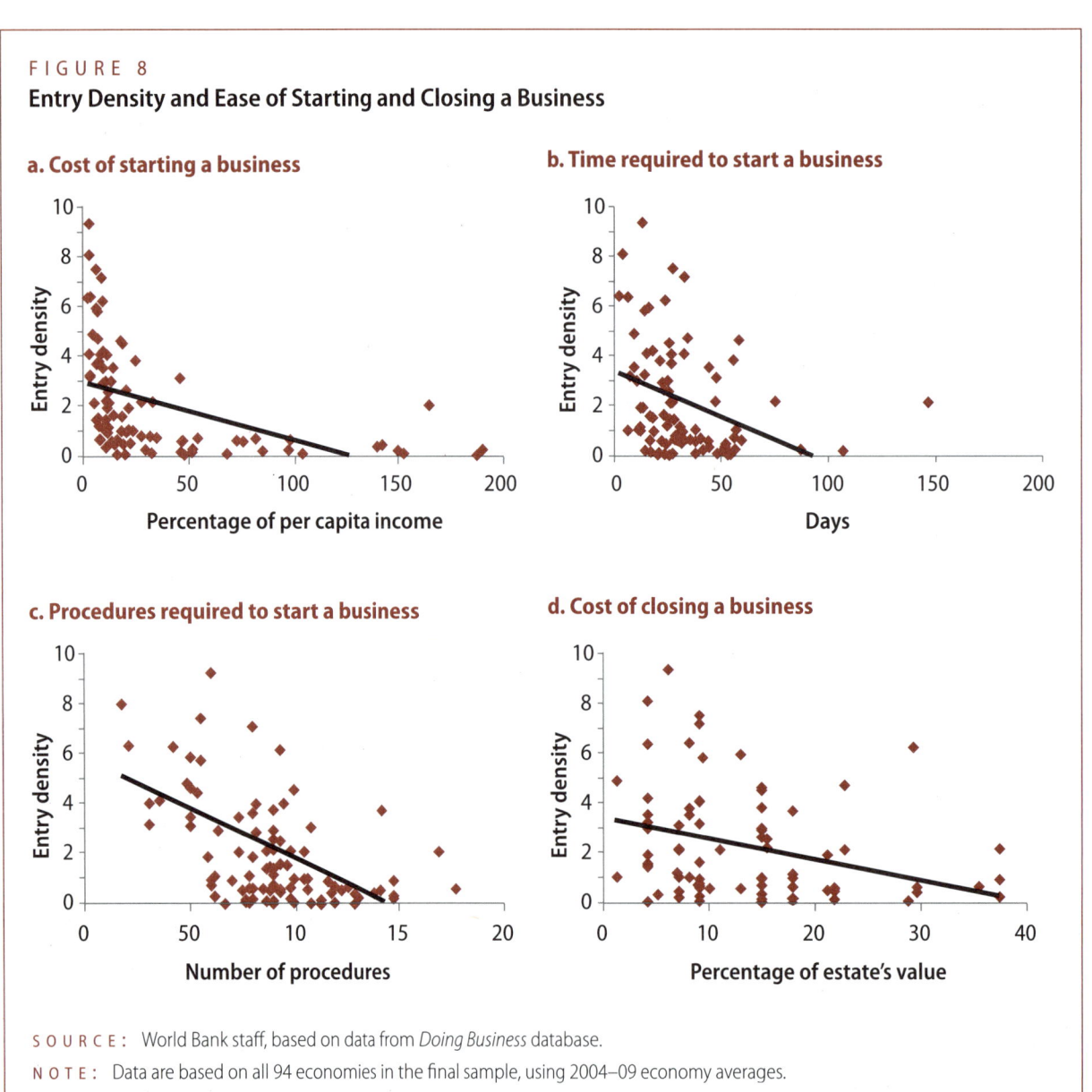

FIGURE 8
Entry Density and Ease of Starting and Closing a Business

a. Cost of starting a business

Entry density vs Percentage of per capita income

b. Time required to start a business

Entry density vs Days

c. Procedures required to start a business

Entry density vs Number of procedures

d. Cost of closing a business

Entry density vs Percentage of estate's value

S O U R C E :   World Bank staff, based on data from *Doing Business* database.

N O T E :   Data are based on all 94 economies in the final sample, using 2004–09 economy averages.

environment variables from 2004 as explanatory variables. The results show that business environment is important for subsequent new business registration, which suggests a causal relationship between initial business environment and

BOX 3

How Has Germany's GmbH Reform Affected New Firm Registration?

On November 1, 2008, Germany introduced a law that created a simplified form of the Gesellschaft mit beschränkter Haftung (GmbH), the most common type of business organization. Under the new law, minimum capital of €25,000 can be paid by setting up a reserve fund that receives 25 percent of the company's profits until the minimum capital amount is reached. Some 12,000 of these new corporations, known as UGs, were registered in 2009, without significant decreases in registrations of other legal forms. Overall, new firm registration increased from 64,840 in 2008 to 73,260 in 2009, an increase of 13 percent.

subsequent registrations. To make sure that the results are driven by the business environment rather than the overall level of development in a country, the analysis controls for GDP per capita, which, as evidenced in figure 7, is also significantly and positively related to entry density. The *Doing Business* indicators remain significant predictors of entry density (Klapper and Love 2010).

In order to account for the economic, political, and financial conditions of the surveyed countries over time, the analysis compares entry density with measures of country-level governance (Kaufmann, Kraay, and Mastruzzi 2006). Panel a of figure 9 shows the strong and positive correlation between entry density and the composite governance index.[15] The governance composite is measured on a scale of –2.5 to 2.5, with higher values indicating better governance. Breaking down the index into its components reveals that the most significant factors affecting new business creation are regulatory quality and government effectiveness.

Comparison of entry density with the corporate tax rate for 77 countries (figure 9, panel b) reveals a strong negative correlation between new firm creation and the tax rate.[16] The strong relationship between entry density and governance and entry density and corporate tax rate are upheld when controlling for the income level of the economy in a multivariate econometric analysis (see Klapper and Love 2010).

Modernization of the Business Registration Process

An important component of the business environment is the business registry itself. Business registries are public entities generally established by commercial or civil code mandates and managed by the ministries of commerce or justice. They are responsible for recording and maintaining

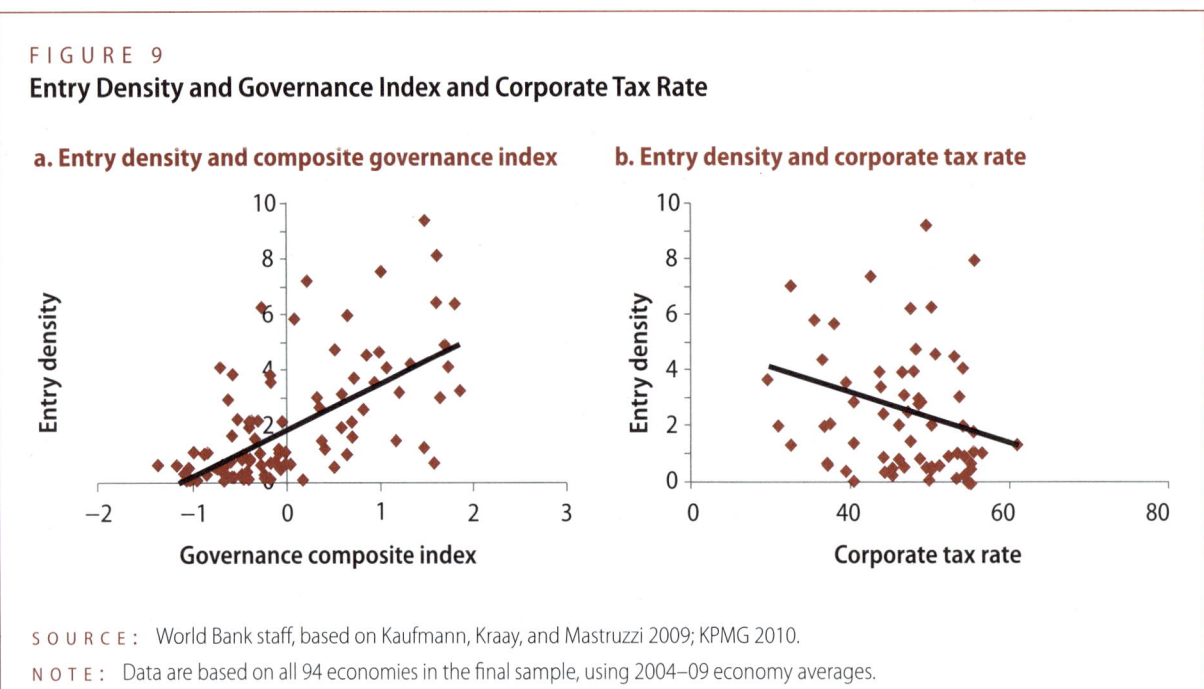

FIGURE 9
Entry Density and Governance Index and Corporate Tax Rate

a. Entry density and composite governance index

b. Entry density and corporate tax rate

S O U R C E : World Bank staff, based on Kaufmann, Kraay, and Mastruzzi 2009; KPMG 2010.

N O T E : Data are based on all 94 economies in the final sample, using 2004–09 economy averages.

certain details on new and existing firms within their jurisdiction, as well as controlling the formation of new firms and the renewal of or changes to existing ones. The main purpose of business registries is to guarantee that businesses comply with regulations and to make such information available to the public. Their composition varies greatly across countries, as evidenced by the fact that they can coexist with real estate (property) registries (as they do in Mexico and Moldova), be managed by chambers of commerce or professional associations (as it is in Syria), or operate as stand-alone agencies (as they

do in the United Kingdom)(World Bank 2009b).[17]

Reforms that improve the business registration processes can spur greater formal sector participation (box 4). They are often implemented as part of a broader private sector reform package (Bruhn 2009). By leveraging information and communication technologies (ICTs), government-to-business e-services and in particular electronic business registries (eBRs) have been shown to increase efficiency, effectiveness, and data reliability and accuracy, as well as to save the time and budgets of company registries and entrepreneurs alike (Hanna 2010; Klapper, Amit, and Guillen 2010).

In addition, eBRs have the potential to deliver "interoperable" government services to entrepreneurs, by, for example, linking business registration with taxation, social services, collateral, and other registrations. Automated online single windows, or one-stop-shops, are good examples of the time and cost savings such interoperability can deliver to both service user and provider. ICTs also offer possibilities for sharing infrastructure, such as government data centers and cloud computing capabilities,

by government agencies, reducing costs and leveraging more advanced technologies than would otherwise have been accessible or affordable.

Responses on ICT–related business entry questions were received from 70 economies, allowing the continuum of business registry technology to be analyzed across the sample. During 2009, the average new entry density was highest in economies in which the complete business registration process was available online (figure 10, panel a). Average new entry density was lowest where no Internet registration was

---

BOX 4

How Did Modernizing Business Registration Systems Affect New Business Registration?

Many economies implemented business registration reforms between 2005 and 2009, often as part of broader private sector reform packages. The impact of these reforms on new business registration was significant. Entry density more than doubled in Belarus after the implementation of a one-stop shop in 2006. El Salvador simplified the legalization of accounting books and publication requirements and lowered the

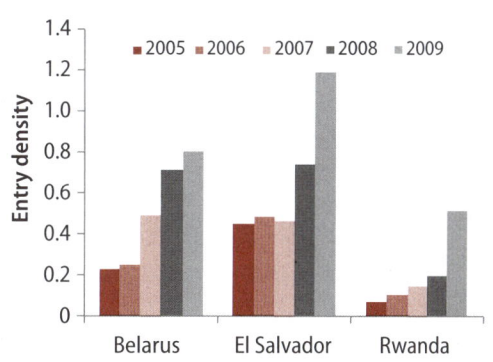

minimum capital requirement. More than 4,400 new firms were registered in El Salvador in 2009, up from 1,680 in 2007. Rwanda saw a 167 percent increase in new firm registration between 2008 and 2009, following the elimination of a notarization requirement, the enablement of online publication, and the consolidation of company registration procedures.

S O U R C E : World Bank staff.

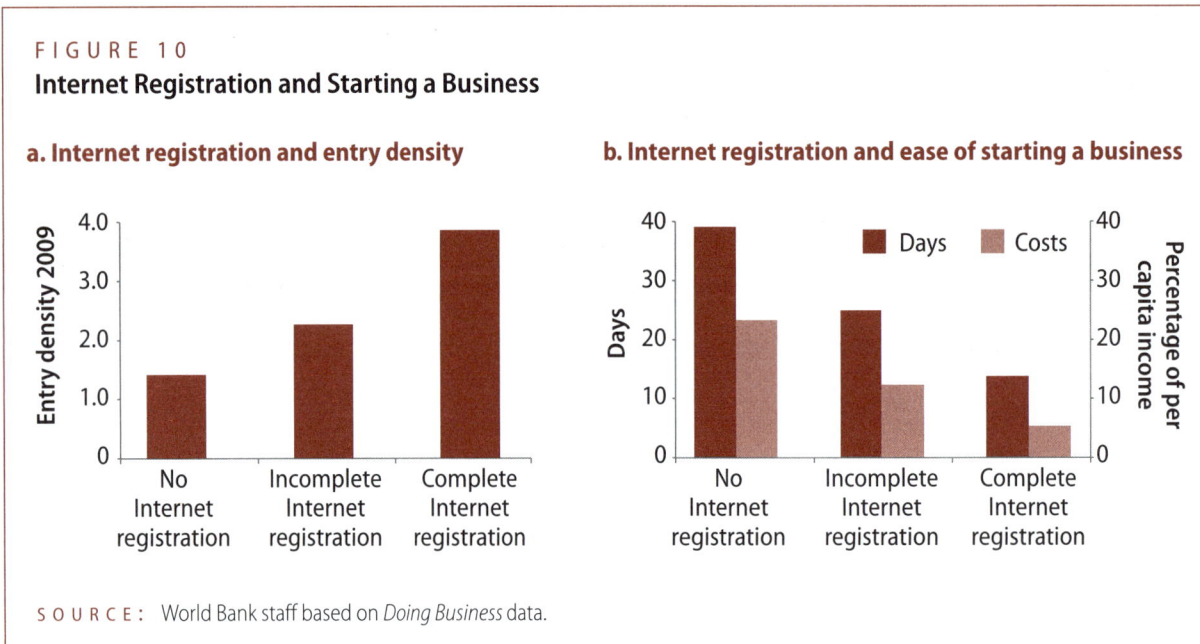

FIGURE 10
Internet Registration and Starting a Business

a. Internet registration and entry density

Entry density 2009

- No Internet registration
- Incomplete Internet registration
- Complete Internet registration

b. Internet registration and ease of starting a business

Days / Percentage of per capita income

■ Days   ■ Costs

- No Internet registration
- Incomplete Internet registration
- Complete Internet registration

SOURCE: World Bank staff based on *Doing Business* data.

possible. Internet registration that also involved nonelectronic steps, such as a notary or in-person document delivery requirements, occupied the middle ground.

Economies in which complete Internet registration is possible had the lowest average starting costs in 2009. Economies in which no Internet registration was possible had the highest cost and required the greatest number of days to start the business. Economies in which Internet registration was possible but required nonelectronic steps again fell in between (figure 10, panel b).

Entrepreneurship and the Financial Crisis

The data show that the lagged and uneven impact of the financial crisis on new firm creation largely mirrors that of the general path of the crisis. The crisis first affected a handful of advanced economies, such as the United States and Iceland, then spread to other economies with highly developed and globally exposed financial systems, particularly those with a reliance on external financing. Last to be affected were emerging economies and those heavily dependent on exports, which suffered as a result of the decline in international trade (see Claessens and others 2010). This section traces the progression of the decline in new firm creation, examines the heterogeneous effect of the crisis on new business registrations, and compares these trends to other measures of turbulence.

New firm creation gradually increased between 2004 and 2007 (see figure 3). The increase was more pronounced in higher-income countries, a trend confirmed by a formal regression model (Klapper and Love 2010). With the onset of the financial crisis in 2008, the trend reversed and entry density declined. The drop occurred first in high- and upper-middle-income economies, a trend confirmed by regression analysis. The crisis also affected new business entry in lower-income groups, although the impact was milder and new entry did not decrease in most lower-middle-income economies until 2009. In many low-income economies, the crisis manifested itself as stagnation rather than a decrease in entry density.

The annual percentage change in new firm registrations offers insight into the impact of the crisis across income groups

(figure 11). High- and upper-middle-income economies experienced the crisis more quickly and more severely than low- and lower-middle-income economies. In 2008 there was almost no growth in new firms in high-income economies, whereas lower-middle and lower-income economies experienced a more than 10 percent increase in new firm registrations. By 2009 every income group of economies-experienced a sharp drop in new firm registration. A few economies did not experience declines in new business registration during the crisis (see raw data in the appendix); as a group, low-income

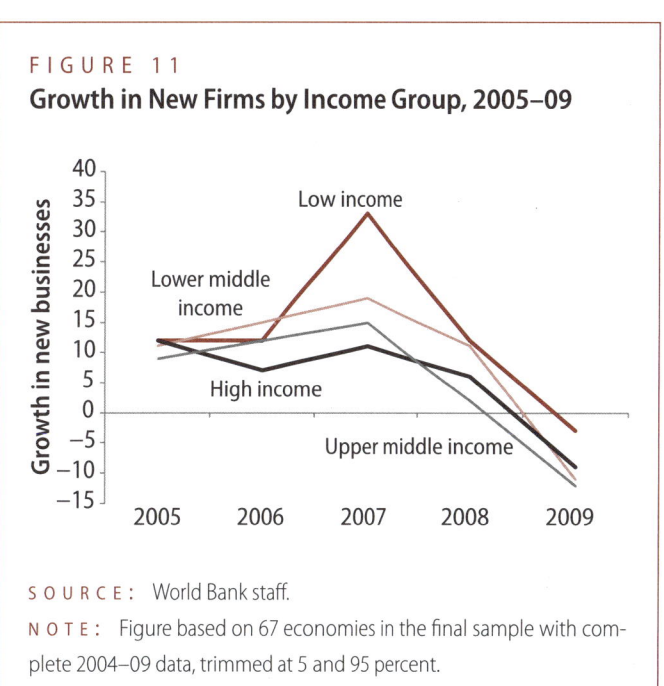

FIGURE 11

Growth in New Firms by Income Group, 2005–09

SOURCE: World Bank staff.

NOTE: Figure based on 67 economies in the final sample with complete 2004–09 data, trimmed at 5 and 95 percent.

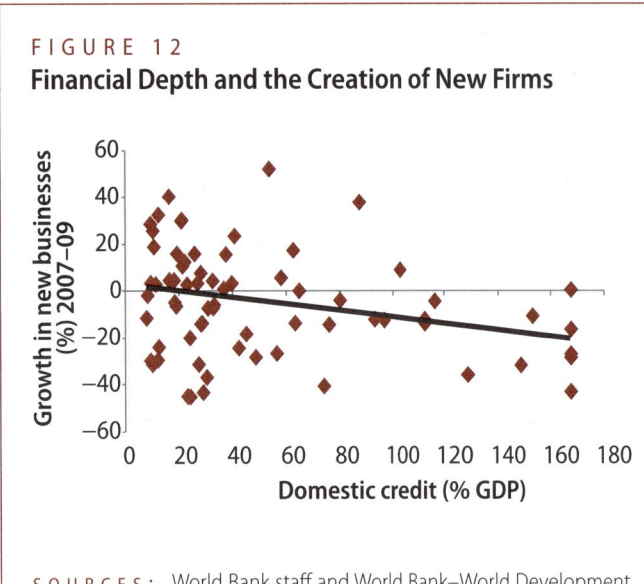

FIGURE 12

Financial Depth and the Creation of New Firms

SOURCES: World Bank staff and World Bank–World Development Indicators statistics.

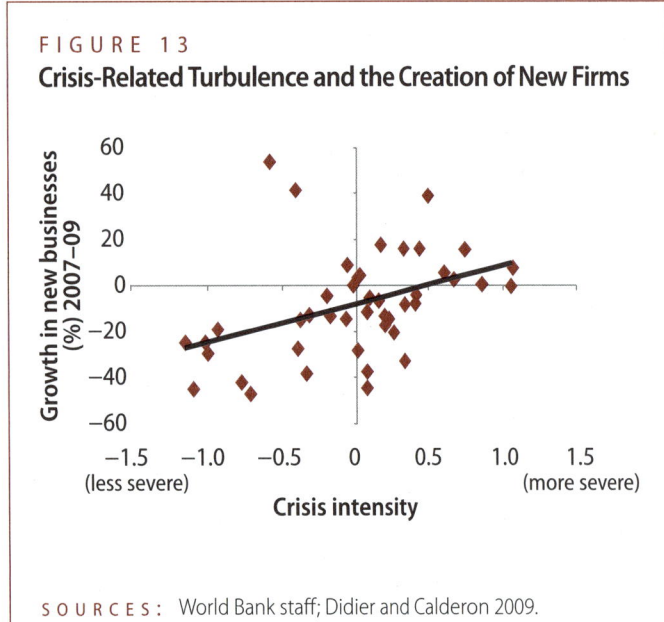

FIGURE 13

Crisis-Related Turbulence and the Creation of New Firms

SOURCES: World Bank staff; Didier and Calderon 2009.

economies experienced the most modest decline in the number of new firms in 2009.

An econometric analysis of the heterogeneous effects of the crisis yields several interesting results. First, economies with higher GDP per capita experienced sharper declines in new registrations during the crisis. This outcome is expected, as the crisis originated primarily in developed economies; it is also consistent with the work of Lane and Milesi-Ferretti (2010), who find that advanced economies were more severely affected than other economies by the crisis. Economies in which financial markets played a larger role in the domestic economy (as measured by the ratio of domestic credit to GDP) also experienced sharper contractions in new firm creation during the crisis (figure 12).

One plausible channel for this result is through firm's access to external finance, which is more important in countries with higher levels of financial development (Rajan and Zingales 1998). This channel suggests that countries in which start-ups are more reliant on and intertwined with banking were more likely to experience larger contractions in new firm creation, as a result of the credit crunch that characterized the financial crisis (that is, where finance is more important for firms, the withdrawal of finance is likely to have a larger negative impact). The results on the impact of financial development are suggestive of this channel. The analysis also reveals that financial development is a more powerful predictor of the impact of the crisis on new firm creation than per capita GDP, which is notable given the high correlation between the two.

The degree to which the crisis affected new firm creation is also highly correlated with measures of crisis severity. Didier and Calderon (2009) develop an index of "turbulence," which measures the degree to which a country was affected by the crisis. Their index of financial turbulence is highly correlated with the percentage change in new firms over the crisis period. Figure 13 shows that countries that were more affected by the financial crisis also experienced the sharpest decline in new firm creation.

The regression analysis confirms the correlation between measures of crisis turbulence and new firm creation. The high vulnerability to the crisis is significantly associated with a drop in new firm creation, even after controlling for the impact of financial development.

Conclusion

The analysis in this report facilitates a more comprehensive examination of the relationship between business creation, business environment, and the recent financial crisis. The findings suggest that dynamic business creation occurs in economies that reduced red tape and provided a stable investment climate. Nearly all economies experienced a sharp drop in business entry during the crisis. The degree to which the crisis affected new firm creation is highly correlated with measures of crisis severity. The data also show that the crisis had more negative impact on new business creation in countries with higher levels of financial development. In future work, these entrepreneurship indicators can be used in conjunction with other measures—such as the *Doing Business* indicators—in the development of policy recommendations to promote private sector development and growth.

Appendix
Entry Density by Economy
2004 – 09

Country	Entry density					
	2004	2005	2006	2007	2008	2009
Albania	0.52	0.53	0.60	0.91	1.24	0.84
Algeria	0.53	0.48	0.40	0.35	0.48	0.44
Argentina	0.56	0.55	0.61	0.62	0.57	0.46
Armenia	1.40	1.22	1.47	1.86	1.72	1.28
Australia	6.61	6.44	5.91	6.38	—	—
Austria	0.60	0.65	0.68	0.66	0.65	0.58
Azerbaijan	0.95	1.05	0.95	0.94	1.22	0.93
Belarus	0.23	0.24	0.25	0.50	0.72	0.80
Belgium	3.70	3.74	4.10	4.46	4.62	4.28
Belize	—	—	—	*4.59*	*4.05*	*3.01*
Bhutan	0.02	0.03	0.03	0.03	0.05	0.04
Bolivia	0.27	0.29	0.32	0.36	0.40	0.43
Bosnia and Herzegovina	—	—	—	0.83	0.58	—
Brazil	1.91	1.94	1.85	2.10	2.40	2.38
Bulgaria	4.63	5.73	6.91	9.81	8.27	7.20
Burkina Faso	0.06	0.07	0.05	0.08	0.07	0.08
Cambodia	0.13	0.18	0.20	0.32	0.30	0.22
Canada	6.54	7.20	8.64	9.13	8.93	7.56
Chile	1.96	2.12	2.31	2.39	2.12	—
Colombia	—	0.92	0.97	1.03	1.10	1.07
Cook Islands	—	—	—	—	*3.24*	*12.30*
Costa Rica	*9.56*	*11.02*	*12.93*	*12.65*	*11.87*	*8.78*
Croatia	2.26	2.72	3.29	3.51	3.36	2.57
Cyprus	*16.55*	*20.05*	*27.30*	*38.17*	*31.47*	*20.30*
Czech Republic	2.00	1.93	2.25	2.87	3.11	3.00
Denmark	4.89	5.87	7.35	7.98	7.09	4.57

Country	Entry density					
	2004	**2005**	**2006**	**2007**	**2008**	**2009**
Dominica	*2.55*	*3.50*	*4.05*	*4.09*	*4.09*	*3.30*
Dominican Republic	—	—	—	—	—	2.13
Egypt, Arab Rep.	0.14	0.09	0.13	0.17	0.13	
El Salvador	—	0.46	0.49	0.47	0.74	1.19
Estonia	6.04	6.85	8.72	8.10	—	—
Ethiopia[a]	0.02	0.02	0.03	0.03	0.03	0.03
Finland	2.46	2.59	2.99	3.93	3.85	3.37
France	2.78	2.86	3.04	3.53	3.52	3.08
Gabon	2.63	3.43	3.21	3.72	5.39	4.27
Georgia	1.06	1.30	1.86	2.22	2.60	2.32
Germany	1.12	1.21	1.19	1.19	1.19	—
Ghana	0.48	0.58	0.59	0.72	—	—
Greece	0.77	0.73	1.06	1.18	—	—
Guatemala	0.65	0.64	0.71	0.70	0.75	0.68
Hong Kong SAR, China	*10.39*	*12.98*	*14.64*	*15.66*	*18.62*	*19.19*
Hungary	3.51	3.22	3.30	4.08	6.41	6.26
Iceland	13.01	14.96	16.01	18.22	12.62	12.84
India	0.05	0.06	0.03	0.07	0.12	—
Indonesia	0.14	0.16	0.16	0.16	0.24	0.18
Ireland	*5.82*	*6.35*	*6.99*	*6.74*	*5.22*	*4.67*
Israel	5.29	4.57	4.41	4.57	4.46	—
Italy	1.81	1.90	1.94	2.01	1.89	1.78
Jamaica	1.08	0.99	1.14	1.16	1.21	1.16
Japan	1.31	1.33	1.73	1.48	1.28	—
Jersey, Channel Islands (UK)	*40.13*	*46.96*	*56.88*	*65.85*	*44.62*	*37.57*
Jordan	0.37	0.58	0.67	0.56	0.64	0.74
Kazakhstan	2.33	2.95	3.13	3.48	2.78	2.59
Kenya	0.35	0.38	0.43	0.79	0.85	—
Korea, Rep.	1.68	0.93	1.89	1.56	1.72	—
Kosovo	0.06	0.16	0.18	0.23	0.11	0.12
Kyrgyz Republic	0.69	0.75	0.88	1.04	1.07	1.26
Latvia	4.62	5.55	7.12	7.64	5.71	4.62

Country	Entry density					
	2004	2005	2006	2007	2008	2009
Liechtenstein	—	—	—	—	44.13	25.11
Lithuania	1.53	1.82	2.14	2.65	2.19	2.18
Luxembourg	*5.71*	*6.27*	*6.98*	*7.38*	—	—
Macedonia, FYR	—	—	5.66	6.55	6.80	5.63
Madagascar	—	—	0.10	0.10	0.11	0.07
Malawi	0.05	0.06	0.06	0.09	0.11	0.08
Malaysia	2.64	2.52	2.51	2.77	2.60	2.55
Maldives	2.90	3.15	3.89	4.05	3.89	3.09
Malta	*9.12*	*8.78*	*10.77*	*9.81*	*9.98*	*9.52*
Mauritius	*5.88*	*7.30*	*8.55*	*10.08*	*10.08*	*7.33*
Mexico[b]	—	0.56	0.59	0.66	0.67	0.61
Moldova	1.40	1.48	1.67	1.93	1.82	1.32
Montenegro	—	—	4.19	5.99	3.89	0.92
Morocco	0.53	0.59	0.90	1.25	1.31	1.28
Netherlands	2.25	2.62	3.26	3.10	3.38	3.10
Netherlands Antilles	*8.40*	*8.45*	*8.68*	*9.41*	*10.09*	*7.99*
New Zealand	23.71	23.54	24.14	27.03	21.59	17.08
Niger	0.01	0.01	0.00	0.00	0.01	0.00
Nigeria	0.32	0.38	0.45	0.59	0.79	0.79
Norway	3.62	4.65	5.95	5.47	4.49	—
Oman	0.72	0.83	1.29	1.87	2.13	1.67
Pakistan	0.03	0.05	0.06	0.05	0.04	0.03
Panama	*3.70*	*6.31*	*0.79*	*4.87*	*2.29*	*0.26*
Peru	1.44	1.69	1.92	2.38	2.71	2.65
Philippines	0.26	0.25	0.24	0.22	0.23	0.19
Poland	—	0.48	0.48	0.50	0.46	0.52
Portugal	3.54	3.68	4.02	4.39	4.51	3.92
Romania	5.80	5.95	5.99	6.62	6.49	3.66
Russian Federation	—	4.95	4.24	4.10	4.22	2.61
Rwanda	0.08	0.08	0.11	0.15	0.20	0.51
Senegal	0.18	0.18	0.20	0.21	0.29	0.22
Serbia	—	2.02	2.14	2.24	2.15	1.94

Country	Entry density					
	2004	2005	2006	2007	2008	2009
Singapore	*5.20*	*5.80*	*6.29*	*7.46*	*7.18*	*7.40*
Slovak Republic	2.63	3.30	3.53	4.01	4.37	4.04
Slovenia	—	2.59	2.75	3.51	4.43	4.16
South Africa	1.25	1.45	1.27	1.14	0.93	0.77
Spain	4.82	5.04	5.42	5.31	3.92	2.92
Sri Lanka	0.30	0.34	0.37	0.32	0.32	0.29
Suriname	0.24	0.53	0.37	0.35	0.54	0.44
Sweden	3.29	3.49	4.04	4.72	4.64	4.09
Switzerland	*2.57*	*1.73*	*4.98*	*3.55*	*2.58*	*4.88*
Tajikistan	0.22	0.21	0.21	0.20	0.24	0.48
Thailand	0.70	0.72	0.67	0.55	0.60	0.59
Togo	—	—	0.01	0.02	0.04	—
Tunisia	0.73	0.80	0.92	1.27	1.14	1.23
Turkey	0.87	0.99	1.08	1.12	0.97	0.87
Uganda	0.55	0.61	0.58	0.60	0.63	0.72
Ukraine	—	0.85	0.97	1.19	0.95	0.60
United Kingdom	9.77	8.30	9.19	11.05	9.11	8.05
Uruguay	3.28	3.46	2.90	3.81	2.92	2.08
Uzbekistan	0.44	0.46	0.54	0.58	0.58	0.78
Vanuatu	*4.49*	*4.07*	*6.60*	*4.45*	*3.46*	*2.18*
Virgin Islands (UK)	*3,718*	*3,486*	*3,804*	*4,389*	*3,449*	*2,605*
Zambia	0.55	0.60	0.62	0.89	1.03	0.88

SOURCE: World Bank staff.

NOTE: Offshore economies in italics. — = Not available.

a. Data for Ethiopia include only federally registered firms.

b. Data for Mexico do not include Mexico City.

Notes

1. Other terms for the registrar of companies include business register (Australia), the registry of commerce (France), companies registration offices (Ireland), public registries of property and commerce (Mexico), mercantile registries (Spain), companies house (the United Kingdom), and incorporation offices (the United States).

2. The appendix contains all of the data in the report.

3. Income groups are according to 2010 World Bank classifications (based on 2008 gross national income per capita).

4. See Shane and Venkataraman (2000) and Venkataraman (1997) for a discussion of alternative definitions.

5. See http://www.census.gov/econ/ for the United States; http://strategis.gc.ca/epic/site/sbrp-rppe.nsf/en/rd00827e.html for Canada; Council Regulation (EEC) No. 696/93 of March 15, 1993, on the statistical units for the observation and analysis of the production system in the European Community, Official Journal L 076, 30/03/1993; and http://www.unece.org/stats/publications/53metadaterminology.pdf for the United Nations Economic Commission on Europe.

6. The registration of businesses without legal entity (professional associations, individual merchants) is voluntary in some countries, such as Spain.

7. The complete data set and sources are available at http://econ.worldbank.org/research/entrepreneurship.

8. The complete list of sources is available at http://econ.worldbank.org/research/entrepreneurship.

9. The Companies Act of Sweden is contained in the Swedish Code of Statutes, SFS 2005:551 (Aktiebolag 2005:551) and the Companies Ordinance in SFS 2005:559. Complete information is available at http://www.notisum.se/Rnp/SLS/lag/20050551.htm.

10. See Firmenbuch Gesetz, Register of Companies Act§ 40 with regard to Austria and http://www.justice.gov.sk for the Slovak Republic.

11. See http://www.rree.gob.pe.

12. See Zoromé (2007) for the complete list of offshore economies: http://www.imf.org/external/np/mae/oshore/2000/eng/back.htm.

13. Data are not available for the entire period for all countries. The period 2004–09 is used in the analysis because it provides the most complete sample.

14. Details on the methodology used for the *Doing Business* indicators can be found at http://www.doingbusiness.org/MethodologySurveys/.

15. The composite governance index aggregates six subindexes: voice and accountability, political stability, government effectiveness, regulatory quality, rule of law, and control of corruption. Complete data are available at info.worldbank.org/governance/wgi/index. asp.

16. Complete data are available at http://www.kpmg.com.sg/publications/Tax_ CorporateIndirectTaxRateSurvey.pdf.

17. The OECD–Eurostat Entrepreneurship Indicators Programme (EIP) has established a framework for using consistent definitions and methodologies to collect indicators of new firm creation across countries. These statistics draw on improved electronic links of information across government agencies to measure the number of active registered firms (Ahmad and Hoffman 2008).

References

Ahmad, N., and A. Hoffman. 2008. "A Framework for Addressing and Measuring Entrepreneurship." OECD Statistics Working Paper 2, Organisation for Economic Co-operation and Development, Paris.

Bruhn, M. 2009. "Does Business Registration Reform Increase Entrepreneurial Activity? Finance and PSD Impact." *The Lessons from DECRG-FP Impact Evaluations*, no. 2 (February).

Busch, Christian, and Lassmann, Andreal. 2010. "Rags to Riches: How Robust Is the Influence of Culture on Entrepreneurial Activity?" KOF Working Paper 267, KOF Swiss Economic Institute, ETH Zurich.

Campello, Murillo, John R. Graham, and Campbell R. Harvey. 2009. "The Real Effects of Financial Constraints: Evidence from a Financial Crisis." Available at SSRN: http://ssrn.com/abstract=1357805.

Chavis, Larry W., Leora F. Klapper, and Inessa Love. 2010. "The Impact of the Business Environment on Young Firm Financing." World Bank Policy Research Working Paper 5322. World Bank, Washington, DC.

Claessens, Stijn, Giovanni Dell'Ariccia, Deniz Igan, and Luc Laeven. 2010. "Cross-Country Experiences and Policy Implications from the Global Financial Crisis." *Economic Policy* 25 (62): 267–93.

Commercial Code of Slovak Republic. Section 68, Act No. 513/1991. Available at http://www.justice.gov.sk.

The Companies Act of Sweden, SFS 2005:551 (Aktiebolag, 2005:551) and the Companies Ordinance, SFS 2005:559. Available at: http://www.notisum.se/Rnp/SLS/lag/20050551.htm.

The Council of the European Communities. Council Regulation (EEC) No. 696/93 of 15 March 1993 on the statistical units for the observation and analysis of the production system in the Community. Official Journal L 076, 30/03/1993 P. 0001–0011.

Demirguc-Kunt, A., I. Love, and V. Maksimovic. 2006. "Business Environment and the Incorporation Decision." *Journal of Banking and Finance* 30 (11): 2967–93.

Didier, T., and C. Calderon. 2009. *Severity of the Crisis and Its Transmission Channels.* LCR Crisis Briefs Series, World Bank, Washington, DC.

Djankov, S., R. La Porta, F. Lopez-de-Silanes, and A. Shleifer. 2002. "The Regulation of Entry." *Quarterly Journal of Economics* 117: 1–35.

Dutta, Roy, and R. Sobel. 2009. "Does the Free Press Nurture Entrepreneurship?" Working Papers 09–12, Department of Economics, West Virginia University, Morgantown, WV.

Galor, O., and M. Stelios. 2006. "The Evolution of Entrepreneurial Spirit and the Process of Development." Working paper, Brown University, Providence, RI.

Gough, J. W. 1969. *The Rise of the Entrepreneur.* New York: Schocken Books.

Haltiwanger, J., R. Jarmin, and J. Miranda. 2009. "Jobs Created from Business Startups in the United States." Kauffman Foundation, Kansas City, MO. January.

Hanna, Nagy. 2010. *Transforming Government and Building the Information Society: Challenges and Opportunities for the Developing World.* New York: Springer.

Jovanovic, B. 1982. "Selection and the Evolution of Industry." *Econometrica* 50: 642–70.

Kaufmann, D., A. Kraay, and M. Mastruzzi, 2006. "Governance Matters V: Governance Indicators for 1996–2005." World Bank Policy Research Working Paper 4012, World Bank, Washington, DC.

———. 2009. "Governance Matters VIII: Aggregate and Individual Governance Indicators, 1996–2008." World Bank Working Paper 4978, World Bank, Washington, DC.

Klapper, L., R. Amit, and R. Guillen. 2010. "Entrepreneurship and Firm Formation across Countries." In *International Differences in Entrepreneurship*, ed. Joshua Lerner and Antoineete Shoar. Chicago: University of Chicago Press.

Klapper, L., L. Laeven, and R. Rajan. 2006. "Entry Regulation as a Barrier to Entrepreneurship." *Journal of Financial Economics* 82 (3): 591–629.

Klapper, L., and I. Love. 2010. "The Impact of the Financial Crisis on New Firm Registration." World Bank Policy Research Working Paper 5444, World Bank, Washington, DC.

Klapper, L., and C. Richmond. 2009. "Patterns of Business Creation, Survival, and Growth: Evidence from a Developing Country." World Bank Working Paper, World Bank, Washington, DC. Mimeo.

KPMG International. 2009. "KPMG's Corporate and Indirect Tax Rate Survey 2009." Amstelveen, Netherlands: KPMG International.

Lane, P. R., and G. M. Milesi-Ferretti. 2010. "The Cross-Country Incidence of the Global Crisis." Unpublished manuscript, International Monetary Fund, Washington, DC.

Longitudinal Employment Analysis Program (LEAP) of Statistics Canada. http://strategis.gc.ca/epic/site/sbrp-rppe.nsf/en/rd00827e.html.

Mullainathan, S., and P. Schnabl. 2009. "Does Less Market Entry Regulation Generate More Entrepreneurs?" In *International Differences in Entrepreneurship*, ed. Joshua Lerner and Antoineete Shoar. Chicago: University of Chicago Press.

Rajan, R., and L. Zingales. 1998. "Financial Dependence and Growth." *American Economic Review* 88 (3): 559–86.

Schmidt, Jessica. 2008. "The New Unternehmergesellschaft (Entrepreneurial Company) and the Limited – A Comparison." *German Law Journal* 1093–1108. http://www.germanlawjournal.com/index.php?pageID=11&artID=990.

Schneider, F., A. Buehn, and C. E. Montenegro. 2010. "Shadow Economies All over the World: New Estimates for 162 Countries from 1999 to 2007." World Bank Policy Research Working Paper No. 5356. World Bank, Washington, DC.

Schneider, F., and D. Enste. 2000. "Shadow Economies: Size, Causes and Consequences." *Journal of Economic Literature* 38 (1): 77–114.

Schumpeter, J. A. 1911. *Theorie Der Wirtschaftlichen Entwicklung.* Leipzig: Duncker and Humblot.

Shane, S., and S. Venkataraman, 2000. "The Promise of Entrepreneurship as a Field of Research." *Academy of Management Review* 25 (1): 217–26.

Stangler, Dane, and Robert E. Litan, 2009. "Where Will the Jobs Come From?" Kauffman Foundation, Kansas City, MO. Mimeo.

United Nations. 2005. "Recommandations internationales concernant les statistiques de l'activité économique." *Commission Économique etr Sociale pour l'Asie et le Pacifique*, E/ESCAP/CPR(2)/9, November.

United Nations Statistical Commission. n.d. "Terminology on Statistical Metadata." Available at http://www.unece.org/stats/publications/53metadaterminology.pdf.

United States Census Bureau. n.d. http://www.census.gov/econ/.

Van Stel, A. J., M. A. Carree, and A. R. Thurik. 2005. "The Effect of Entrepreneurial Activity on National Economic Growth." *Small Business Economics* 24: 311–21.

Venkataraman, S. 1997. "The Distinctive Domain of Entrepreneurship Research: An Editor's Perspective." In *Advances in Entrepreneurship, Firm Emergence, and Growth*, Vol. 3, ed. J. Katz and R. Brockhouse: 119–38. Stamford, CT: JAI Press.

Wennekers, S., A. van Stel, R. Thurik, and P. Reynolds. 2005. "Nascent Entrepreneurship and the Level of Economic Development." *Small Business Economics* 24: 293–309.

World Bank. 2009a. *Doing Business 2010*. Washington, DC: World Bank.

———. 2009b. *Information and Communications for Development: Extending Reach and Increasing Impact*. Washington, DC: World Bank.

Zoromé, A. 2007. "Concept of Offshore Financial Centers: In Search of an Operational Definition." IMF Working Paper 07/87, International Monetary Fund, Washington, DC.

ECO-AUDIT
Environmental Benefits Statement

The World Bank is committed to preserving endangered forests and natural resources. The Office of the Publisher has chosen to print **Entrepreneurship Snapshots 2010** on recycled paper with 100 percent postconsumer fiber in accordance with the recommended standards for paper usage set by the Green Press Initiative, a nonprofit program supporting publishers in using fiber that is not sourced from endangered forests. For more information, visit www.greenpressinitiative.org.

Saved:
- 3 trees
- 1 million British thermal units of total energy
- 246 pounds of net greenhouse gases (CO_2 equivalent)
- 3,325 gallons of waste water
- 310 pounds of solid waste